DOGOLOGY

This edition published in 2021
By SJG Publishing, HP22 6NF, UK

Author: Michael Powell
Cover design: Milestone Creative
Contents design: seagulls.net

ISBN: 978-1-913004-16-3

Printed in China

10 9 8 7 6 5 4 3 2 1

Contents

Introduction	4
It's a dog's life in your hands	6
Your dog's emotional world	9
Why play is important	12
Social skills	15
Bonding and trust	18
How clever are dogs?	21
How do dogs learn?	24
Stimulate your dog's brain	27
What does your dog remember?	30
It's all in the eyes	33
Telltale tails	36
Extraordinary senses	39
Ears in action	42
A medley of barks	45
Facial expressions	48
Body language	51
Do dogs need their whiskers?	54
Unique communication	57
Jumping Up	60
Clues your dog loves you	63
The joy of giving	66
Why so needy?	69
A fascination with sticks	72
To sleep, perchance to dream	75
Tearing up the rules	78
Embarrassing canine habits	81
Stress, anxiety and depression	84
Signs your dog is unwell	87
Elderly dogs	91
What can we learn from dogs?	94

INTRODUCTION

Dogology is the art and science of the mind and behaviour, instincts and intentions, hopes and dreams, quirks, foibles and misdemeanours of the domesticated carnivoran of the family Canidae, otherwise known as – our dumb-smart, eternally-loyal mud-magnets – dogs.

At home, at work or at play, on the sofa or lying curled up under the kitchen table licking peanut butter from a rubber toy, anyone can become an expert dogologist, so long as they have an open and loving heart, the curiosity to learn about the irrepressible canine psyche and a willingness to view the world from a dog's perspective.

We hope this little book will encourage you to understand, communicate more effectively with and nurture all the dogs in your life, during the short time you spend together and fuels a burning desire to enable them to be healthy, happy and above all – uniquely themselves.

IT'S A DOG'S LIFE IN YOUR HANDS

Dog owners strive to give their dogs the best lives they possibly can, during the relatively short time that they share the planet with us. They join our families, fill our hearts and then all too soon they are gone. So, what is the single most important thing that you can do for your canine friend while you enjoy this precious time together?

Actually, the answer is very simple, but it's not what you might think. Let's take it as a given that you want your dog to have a happy, secure, healthy and long life. The key is how you can achieve all those things. For example, the answer isn't 'love your dog, unconditionally', nor is it 'show him who's boss, because dogs need that'. Both of those aims have their merits and their pitfalls. You can't love an animal and do what's best for them if you know nothing about them. You need a knowledge base. Likewise, although it's true that dogs prefer you to be the leader, showing him who's boss has the wrong kind of energy and motivation and it harks back to methods of dog training that have become increasingly discredited and are now widely viewed as harmful bullying.

The more ethologists (scientists who study animal behaviour) learn about dogs, the more complexity they uncover. Animal behaviourist Alexandra Horowitz makes this important observation in the first chapter of her book, *Inside of a Dog*: 'What we'll find, in looking at dogs through a scientific lens, is that some of what we think we know about dogs is entirely borne out; other things that appear patently true are, on closer examination, more doubtful than we thought'.

One of the most important things you can do is to try to see things from your dog's point of view to understand what he wants. We dog lovers think we know lots about dogs just because we love them and assume that's more than halfway to understanding them. But the truth is that sometimes the way we treat our animals, often with the best intentions, is just plain wrong. For example, many dog owners, either verbally or physically, punish their dogs for growling, especially when they are in public, where they feel a social pressure to be seen to be in control and teaching their dogs how to 'behave'.

A dog who growls isn't a bad dog – he's actually a very good dog who is communicating, in the only way he knows, that he is feeling uncomfortable with a situation. Far from being rude or aggressive, a growl is a polite warning that communicates a dog's desire to de-escalate. Dogs always try to avoid physical confrontation and they've developed a sophisticated system of vocalisation and body language in order to achieve that.

Unless your dog growls at you playfully during a game of tug-of-war, for example, he is usually giving you a polite warning to back off. If you ignore him, the next step may well be a bite. If you scold or punish a growl, rather than understand its intention, the next time your dog feels threatened, he will skip the growl – which you have taught him is ineffective – and go straight for the bite. And no doubt he'll get punished for that and so begins a repeat cycle that leaves the dog confused, misunderstood and wrongly labelled as 'dangerous'.

So, how do we become less prone to making these mistakes? The key is to keep building our knowledge base whilst recognising more fully the differences between our two species, rather than assume that our unique bond and good intentions will always guide us to do the right thing. Ideally, the information in this book will confirm some of what you already know, but also help you become aware of some of your misconceptions. Alexandra Horowitz again: 'The way around this kind of misstep is to replace our anthropomorphising instinct with a behaviour-reading instinct. In most cases, this is simple: we must ask the dog what he wants. You need only know how to translate his answer'.

YOUR DOG'S EMOTIONAL

You don't have to be a dog owner to understand that dogs have emotions and they aren't exactly in the business of hiding them (except maybe when they are injured). When a dog is happy or sad, angry or contented, she lets us know about it. It seems so obvious that dogs have an emotional inner life, but it wasn't always this way.

Centuries ago, when we lived in agrarian communities and it could be said that we were more in touch with the natural world, humans formed close relationships with dogs. The existence of their emotions would have been self-evident, just as it is for us today. However, as Stanley Coren explains in his book *Do Dogs Dream?*, during the sixteenth and seventeenth centuries, 'scientists were learning that living things are composed of systems that follow chemical and mechanical rules'. The French philosopher René Descartes suggested that 'animals like dogs are simply some kind of machine, filled with the biological equivalent of gears and pulleys'. Thirty years after Descartes' death, the French rationalist philosopher Nicolas Malebranche argued that all ideas existed only in God and that all human action was entirely dependent on God. With such a grim view about human self-determination, it was unsurprising that his view on animals was that they 'eat without pleasure, cry without pain, act without knowing it: they desire nothing, fear nothing, know nothing'.

Science and religion were jointly responsible for the spread of this mechanistic view of humans and animals, but we have the Victorians to thank for placing the modern dog at the heart of the family home. Dogs – especially pet miniatures – were hugely popular with wealthy Victorians, who pampered, dressed them up, anthropomorphised them and viewed them as the embodiment of desirable cultural values such as loyalty and courage. When dogs died they were mourned by their owners and buried in pet cemeteries with gravestones.

Today, with our understanding of modern neurochemistry, 'we have now come to understand that dogs possess all of the same brain structures that produce emotions in humans. Dogs have the same hormones and undergo the same chemical changes that humans do during emotional states' says Stanley Coren. We also know that dogs produce oxytocin and studies have shown that levels of this 'love' hormone increase in humans and dogs when we spend time together.

However, Coren stresses that dogs do not possess the full range of emotions of humans: 'Just like a two-year-old child, our dogs clearly have emotions, but many fewer kinds of emotions than found in adult humans'. At birth, a human baby has one emotion – excitement, which soon branches off into contentment and distress, followed a few months later by disgust, fear and anger, then joy, shyness and suspicion and finally, at about nine months of age, love. This is as far as a dog's emotions reach.

Dogs do not possess the full range of emotions of humans

Depending on the rate of maturation of the breed, 'dogs go through their developmental stages much more quickly than humans do and have all of the emotional range that they will ever achieve by the time they are four to six months of age'.

Dogs don't feel shame or guilt. They may look guilty after they have soiled the carpet or destroyed a prized possession, but that's really just an expression of fear because they know from past experience that bad things happen when they break your rules. Dogs don't feel pride or contempt – and that's why you'll never meet a narcissistic or spiteful dog.

At about three years of age, humans develop shame and pride, and guilt about six months later. Contempt doesn't appear until about age four. No wonder we talk about the innocence of youth and the blithe, adorable nature of dogs.

WHY PLAY IS *IMPORTANT*

Dogs show each other that they are friendly and want to play by performing a play bow – with head lowered and front legs flat on the ground to the elbow, while the backside remains upright, tail wagging. If a dog is really excited, he will perform several play bows in a row and jump around in between.

Puppies are naturally playful and any interaction with your puppy can easily turn into a play session, which performs several important functions. For example, if you gently push your puppy onto her back and let her roll her legs while you rub her tummy, this is fun play that gives her exercise, promotes trust and bonding, shows your dominance, establishes boundaries and teaches her that you can touch any part of her body without being a threat. She will probably respond by playfully mouthing your hand or trying to play tug-of-war with your clothing. Discourage this behaviour by substituting your hand or clothing for one of her toys, so that the fun can continue. This teaches her that while she may play with other dogs with full contact, human body parts are not for chewing, even playfully.

Most dogs love to play tug-of-war, but some experts claim it is harmful because it teaches the dog to fight you and that you mustn't let your dog win because that demonstrates their dominance. But there are so many benefits to tug-of-war, not least that it helps your dog to feel grounded and it is an opportunity to teach her how to play rough whilst setting safe boundaries. For example, if she accidentally nips your hand, or lunges at you too boisterously, either make a little yelp, to show her that she has caused you pain, or stop playing until she's calmed down. She will quickly learn how to play safely and she will soon initiate play by bringing toys to you.

Some dog trainers advise that tug-of-war should stop if the dog growls, which is probably the best advice for children, but lots of dogs growl playfully and most responsible adult owners can make their own judgement call.

Other less controversial and more co-operative games include retrieving objects or playing hide-and-seek with them, or teaching your dog the names of her various toys and getting her to fetch them for you. This will naturally offer lots of scope for success and praise (don't make it too hard, play should be fun not frustrating) and lots of stroking, rubbing and nuzzling, all the while teaching your puppy to feel safe when you are touching her. Be kind. Don't taunt your dog by making her fail all the time or making her really confused or, worst of all, turning her into an object of ridicule.

Hide-and-seek never gets boring. Hide somewhere in your house and then call your dog to come. Naturally, you will give your dog lots of praise or even a doggy treat when she finds you. You can also hide dog treats around the house and then go on a hunt together; she'll have great fun sniffing them out and, if she's clueless, you can point her in the right direction.

Always try to accept your dog's invitation to play, otherwise she will learn that you are no fun and will eventually stop asking. Make sure your dog has a good selection of toys, so she can amuse herself. Many dogs love ripping apart their stuffed toys, but make sure they don't swallow the stuffing. Rubber toys are generally much more durable and the ones you can fill with treats or peanut butter can keep a dog occupied for a long time.

Don't forget that training is also a form of play, or at least it should be if you're doing it right. Victoria Stilwell, television presenter and author of *It's Me or the Dog*, explains: 'When I am showing owners how to teach their dogs basic commands, usually they're very serious … when we get to ROLL OVER … everyone laughs and it's all very playful. But training should be like that all the time'.

SOCIAL
Skills

Domestic dogs are very skilled at reading human social and communicative behaviour – even more so than our nearest primate relatives – and some have even been bred to use specific human gestures. For example, when a Pointer wants to communicate to humans the location of game, he stands still and aims his muzzle in its direction.

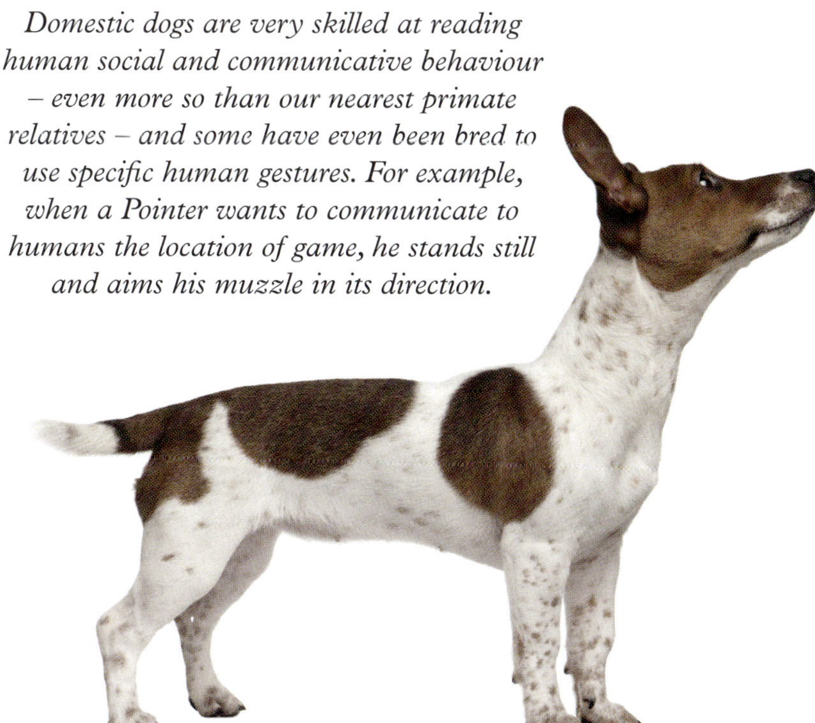

Research led by the professor of evolutionary anthropology at Duke University in North Carolina in the US, Brian Hare, and evolutionary psychologist Professor Michael Tomasello, published in the scientific journal, *Trends in Cognitive Sciences*, argues that recent comparisons between canid species 'suggest that these unusual social skills have a heritable component and initially evolved during domestication as a result of selection on systems mediating fear and aggression towards humans'.

These human-like forms of co-operation and communication are an example of what scientists call 'co-operative evolution' – the process where groups of organisms work or act together for common or mutual benefits.

'Wolves and dogs are actually quite similar when they're very young: They both do the same playful behaviour, run around in circles, and generally look cute. Little wolf puppies will even bark like a dog,' says Nicholas Dodman, professor emeritus and former head of the Animal Behaviour Clinic at the Cummings School of Veterinary Medicine at Tufts University in the US. 'But suddenly the wolf grows up and becomes aloof and lean and suspicious'.

It has been widely assumed that humans domesticated wolves, but in *National Geographic Magazine*, in an article entitled 'We Didn't Domesticate Dogs. They Domesticated Us', Brian Hare and Vanessa Woods argue the opposite, the 'scavenger hypothesis': 'Most likely, it was wolves that approached us, not the other way around … The wolves that were bold but aggressive would have been killed by humans, and so only the ones that were bold and friendly would have been tolerated'.

As discussed on page 44, as friendlier wolves co-existed with humans, they started to look and think differently, their muzzles, jaws and tails shrank, their fur lightened, eyes became bigger and more expressive, their faces cuter. Most important of all, 'these protodogs evolved the ability to read human gestures ... Even our closest relatives – chimpanzees and bonobos – can't read our gestures as readily as dogs can'.

Domestication has created dogs with two skills vital for co-operative problem solving with humans: *social tolerance* – allowing a potential partner to come close, even where there is competition for food; and *social attentiveness* – paying sufficient attention to one's partners in order to adapt one's own behaviour and co-operate. In short, a dog's ability to tolerate humans and to pay attention to us has enabled a hard-wired channel of communication to grow between our two species.

The advantage gained by hunting with dogs is beyond dispute

There is some debate about whether humans actually learned to follow, herd and hunt big game from wolves, but the advantage gained by hunting with dogs is beyond dispute.

In their book, *The Genius of Dogs*, Hare and Woods discuss the likelihood of *mutual domestication*: 'Humans who were tolerant of proto-dogs would have been better off than those who were not. More tolerant and less aggressive humans could maximize the benefit' of having dogs as hunting partners and protectors, which would have generated more plentiful resources and would have allowed for even greater tolerance and sharing. Humans have been as strongly affected by our relationship with dogs as they have been by their relationship with us: 'Dogs may even have been the catalyst for our civilization'.

BONDING AND

There is no comparable bond between two separate species in the entire animal kingdom as that between humans and domesticated dogs. It is a remarkable success story that has been told for up to 32,000 years of partnership and domestication. Humans have bred dogs for hunting, herding, protection and companionship, but also for loyalty and emotional support.

You owe a debt to the millions of humans and dogs who have preceded you and developed this unique symbiosis over millennia. Your dog is hard-wired to bond with you, so whether you get him as an eight-week-old puppy, or rescue an older dog and give him a second home, there are lots of things you can do to encourage an ever-deepening bond and trust.

Most dogs tend to bond with whoever gives them the most positive attention, although certain breeds – such as Basenji, Greyhound, Shiba Inu, Cairn Terrier and Viszla – tend to form a strong bond with a single person. Have faith, even during those early days of gaining your dog's trust and co-operation, that so long as you meet his needs, make him feel safe, treat him at all times with compassion and respect, give him routine, dependability, a bit of training and lots of play, although the speed varies between breeds and individuals, a bond will develop organically.

Signs of a weak bond include emotional indifference to you and the family, your dog doesn't respond to commands (especially the recall command), lack of interest in playing, doesn't like being handled, tries to run away, has poor focus and eye contact, shows aggression, depression or lethargy.

A recently rescued dog may take several months to adjust to the separation from his previous owner and may display weak bonding, but equally, with some rescue dogs or a young puppy, you may be lucky enough to experience this mutual connection within a few days. Even so, homing any dog takes a lot of work and, in common with raising a human baby, initially it can feel like a thankless task and that you are doing all the giving without getting enough back in return.

Hang in there and trust that the bond will form and that soon you will see that special light in his eyes when he sees you, he'll check in with you on walks rather than running off, he will have a desire to be near you, enjoy physical interaction, he will come when you call and will show a strong desire to communicate his needs and wants to you.

In turn, you will soon instinctively understand what he is trying to tell you (for example, if he waits by the door, you will know he wants to be let out, or he might jump up onto the sofa for a cuddle when he needs reassurance). It is not true that all dogs hate to be kissed or even loosely hugged; many dog breeds thrive on and openly invite close human contact.

To strengthen the bond, supply lots of one-to-one attention and activity, which can include obedience and agility training and other fun activities such as hiking, exploring the woods, going to the beach and playing games, which give him exercise and improve communication. Work on the recall command and give him lots of praise and dog treats when he comes back to you. Teach him that good things happen when he is in your company. Socialise him with lots of other dogs and humans, so that he gains trust and confidence and starts to learn that the outside world can be full of positive and fun experiences. Groom and pet him regularly so he learns to enjoy physical contact and trusts your touch.

Any training should be motivated by the desire to keep him and those around him safe, not as an exercise in bending him to your will. On our dog walks we've all encountered those troubling dog owners who seem to demand unswerving obedience at all costs from their animals, who appear to lack joy as they constantly bark reprimands and see their dog as a potential threat rather than as a friend and companion who thrives on firm but compassionate guidance.

HOW CLEVER ARE DOGS?

People often cite the benchmark of a two-and-a-half-year-old human child when discussing the intelligence of dogs. Researchers have found that, on average, dogs are capable of understanding up to 250 words and gestures, can count up to five and perform simple mathematical calculations – which is one way of measuring.

Of course, there will always be exceptions. John Pilley, a retired American psychology professor, spent years training and testing the intelligence of his female border collie, Chaser, until she could understand more than 1,000 words and identify by name every item in a collection of 1,022 objects, which included 800 stuffed animals, 116 balls and 26 frisbees.

Other dogs have shown a similar ability for learning words, and while these feats of super learning are unusual, dogs in general have been shown to learn and recall new words more quickly than primates, including chimps and bonobos. This can be explained by a dog's *social intelligence* – they learn more quickly because dogs are bonded with their human teachers and are highly motivated to please them and co-operate, more so than the primates.

Journalist Bradley Blackburn, writing for *ABC News*, explains: 'Some researchers hypothesize that over tens of thousands of years of domestication, dogs have developed a humanlike social learning ability'. Dogs have been bred over centuries to develop this special attention to words.

In his book *The Intelligence of Dogs*, psychology professor Stanley Coren ranked more than 100 dog breeds based on three specific types of intelligence: *instinctive intelligence* (ability to perform tasks it was bred to perform like herding or hunting); *adaptive intelligence* (ability to independently problem solve and learn from previous experiences) and *working and obedience intelligence* (ability to learn from humans). He ranked the top ten smartest breeds in descending order: Border Collie, Poodle, German Shepherd, Golden Retriever, Doberman Pinscher, Shetland Sheepdog, Labrador Retriever, Papillon, Rottweiler and Australian Cattle Dog. He ranked the least smartest dog breed as the Afghan Hound, followed in increasing intelligence by Basenji, Bulldog,

Chow Chow, Borzoi, Bloodhound, Pekingese and Mastiff, Beagle and Basset Hound.

If you own an Afghan Hound you'll recognise the common assertion that they are difficult to train, but you also love them because of their high self-esteem and independence. You'll probably be the first to argue that measuring dog intelligence is highly subjective, considering the vast differences in skill sets among various breeds, each of which has been bred for specific tasks, and so ease of training may not be an accurate way to assess a dog's intelligence.

All dogs have different skills and they excel in their own fields. Afghan Hounds are excellent hunters. Basset Hounds are better than other dogs at tracking scents, but they are considered to be hard to train because, as Nicholas Dodman explains, 'they don't really look up, they look down. They're not really interested in listening or pleasing anybody, they're just interested in tracking with their noses'. Like the aforementioned chimps and bonobos, they are less motivated to co-operate with humans.

Professor Brian Hare agrees that dog intelligence is highly subjective: 'I don't really think there is any such thing as smart dogs and dumb dogs,' he states. 'That is just a throwback to a linear version of intelligence, as though intelligence is a cup of coffee that is more or less full. Different dogs are good at different things. And all of them are geniuses in their own way'.

Another question that many dog owners think they already know the answer to is: Are dogs smarter than cats? At last science has the answer: Yes! A team led by neurologist Suzana Herculano-Houzel has used a recently developed post-mortem technique to estimate the number of neurons in the cerebral cortex of animal brains. They counted 500 million neurons in a dog's brain, which is double the 250 million they measured in the brains of cats.

HOW DO DOGS LEARN?

Dogs, like children, learn best by positive reinforcement, a simple technique that rewards desired ('good') behaviour and ignores undesired ('bad') behaviour. This seems obvious, but many dog owners give so much attention to unwanted behaviour that they reinforce the very thing they want to eradicate.

The key to learning is good communication and this doesn't just mean barking orders and bending your dog to your will. Sure, you can get results like that, by exploiting the trust that makes our dogs so lovable and loyal. But you'll also create a cowed and anxious dog, who obeys you out of fear rather than willingly with happiness, confidence, love and … dog treats.

Positive reinforcement: Most dogs want to please. It's hardwired into their DNA. But we are not the only thing competing for their attention. For example, if you want your dog to return to you when you're in the park, give her a dog treat as soon as she comes back, every time, otherwise her desire to get a longer walk by disobeying you will inevitably win out.

Reward small steps: If you want to teach your dog a more complicated skill such as retrieving, then you must break it down into its component parts and reward your dog for each step she takes that takes her closer to the goal. For example, if you throw a ball and she just catches it but doesn't come back, reward her at first for the catch, then once she associates this behaviour with a reward 100% of the time, remove the reward until she figures out the next step, which might be as little as taking a couple of steps towards you after she has caught the ball. Once you have consolidated this new behaviour with treats, withdraw the reward once again until she has another breakthrough, and so on, until the goal is reached.

Error-free learning: You must also be consistent at all times, offering your dog lots of mental stimulation and exercise and helping her to succeed by changing her environment to reduce her opportunities to screw up (e.g. whose fault is it if she snaffles the

> Most dogs want to please. It's hardwired into their DNA.

roast chicken you left within her reach, or if she chewed your best shoes because you didn't put them safely away?).

Establish yourself as leader: If you want a co-operative, obedient and happy dog who is willing to learn, then you must be the leader. Some breeds of dog are naturally more dominant than others and a hierarchy is quickly established within a new litter of puppies, but nearly all dogs in a home environment are more secure and settled when they are not burdened by the responsibility of being the leader.

Imagine if your dog believed it was her sole duty to keep you safe. Now imagine the stress and confusion she would feel every time you left the house. She wouldn't know where you were or whether you needed help. All she would know is that she had no control, so she would become anxious and might start tearing up the furniture in your absence. Upon your return, this seemingly wilful damage might cause you to lose your temper and start shouting at the dog to 'teach' her that she has done wrong, or even worse, resort to physical correction – causing your poor dog even greater confusion and fear. Wrong, wrong, wrong. You are solely to blame.

A leader stays calm, exudes calm authority, and nurtures and protects the dogs in his or her care and teaches them good manners. For example, if your dog jumps up to greet you, as leader you should ignore her until she calms down, so that she interacts with you on your terms not hers. You keep your dog physically below you. You may decide that she can sleep on the sofa, but don't let her sit on your shoulder. It isn't cute. It teaches the dog that you are a doormat.

STIMULATE YOUR DOG'S
Brain

In his book, Think Dog, *canine expert John Fisher says it is the responsibility of the owner to 'provide positive physical and mental stimulation. Training, play and exercise should be part of daily life, not optional extras'. The key here is 'daily'. This stimulation of brain and body should be as solid a routine as feeding.*

Dogs thrive on consistency, so it messes with their wellbeing when they spend their days lying around patiently waiting for those moments of excitement and wondering whether there will even be any fun today. We have no problem setting up a feeding routine, because we recognise that dogs need feeding every day, but it's important to understand that mental and physical stimulation are also daily necessities, not optional luxuries.

You don't need a PhD in canine behaviour to provide stimulation, you just need to interact with your dog regularly and consistently, so that he doesn't spend the whole day feeling bored and uncertain. Most dog owners do this instinctively because messing around with dogs is fun, but it's those times when you are too busy to give your dog the attention he deserves that you really need to dig deep and put his needs before your own timetable. Of course, it's forgivable to have the odd lapse and have a hectic day in which the dog barely gets a look in, but unless you set firm rules for yourself and have the discipline to follow them, it's all too easy for busy days to turn into busy weeks and before long, cheating your dog of his basic daily needs becomes the norm. Feeling guilty about it is no substitute for changing your behaviour so that you always aim to put your dog first.

There are lots of different ways to stimulate your dog's brain – playing, learning, problem solving (hiding toys or treats), obedience (safety) training, learning tricks, interesting and varied walks offering lots of opportunities for him to interact with humans, dogs and his environment. Your dog also has a rich emotional life and experiences major emotions such as excitement, fear and anger, represented by basic neural chemistry that is very similar to our own, although he doesn't suffer the human condition of being able to make a negative emotion worse by ruminating. In that respect, dogs obey the cliché that they live very much in the moment. In fact, if you can regularly lose yourself in the moment whenever you play with your dog, then your own wellbeing will see a significant improvement.

So, it's no surprise that regular and consistent stimulation is the key to having an emotionally well-balanced, socially confident, happy and healthy dog, and that many negative behaviours can be blamed on a lack of sufficient stimulation. Your dog's wellbeing is a mirror that reflects your own vital connection to the world around you. The best dog owners live their lives to the full, they are physically active, they have goals and challenges and they make strong emotional connections with other humans, animals and with nature. If your dog lacks stimulation, or if you suspect that you have a bored dog, recognise that you have created that situation. The richness of your dog's life is entirely your responsibility and whatever he is lacking is a strong indicator that, even though you may have a very busy and active schedule, your own work-life balance may be dysfunctional.

One way your dog will express a need for greater stimulation is by engaging in compulsive behaviours such as increased barking, chewing, digging, pacing or following you around. Bored dogs often destroy your stuff and make a mess! If your dog attacks the sofa or shreds your favourite pair of shoes, or you're sick of collecting chewed stick fragments from the lawn, instead of punishing, reward him by giving him more attention.

Stimulation isn't about turning your dog into a genius or teaching him a repertoire of tricks to entertain you and show off to your friends. It's about living fully in the world with your dog and integrating this family member completely into your daily life.

WHAT DOES YOUR DOG
Remember?

To acquire the skills of object permanence (does an object still exist when it is removed from view?), learning (if you always hide food underneath the same of two cups, will he learn the pattern?) and problem solving (figuring out how to get the treat), memory would appear to be an integral part of all three of these classic measures of so-called intelligence. But despite anecdotal evidence that dogs remember their owners after years of separation, their performance in formal tests is mixed.

Many decades ago, Swiss psychologist Jean Piaget established object permanence as a key stage in child development. If you show a one-year-old child a toy and then hide it behind a screen, most understand that the toy can be found behind the screen. Dogs also have no trouble looking behind the screen to find it. However, when two screens are introduced and dogs are actually shown that the toy has been taken out of a container and left behind the first screen, they still look for it in the empty container that has come to rest behind the second screen.

However, Alexandra Horowitz, author of *Inside a Dog*, says the dog's behaviour points to two explanations. The first is that a dog's relationship to objects is fairly limited – they either play with them or eat them: 'neither interaction requires complex rumination on the object. Dogs realise when a previously treasured object is missing, but needn't mull over possible stories for what happened to it'. They simply start sniffing it out with their super powerful noses or wait for it to turn up.

A dog's relationship to objects is fairly limited – they either play with them or eat them

'The second explanation is more far-reaching,' Horowitz explains. Dogs tend to look to humans for cues, and so any test that involves a human will return a biased result because, 'when presented with a problem of any kind, dogs cleverly look to us … they have succeeded magnificently. They have applied a novel tool to the task. We are that tool'.

We know that dogs remember lots of details. They can be taught to obey dozens of commands and some dogs have shown an extraordinary ability to remember the names of hundreds of toys.

This is known as semantic memory. They also possess strong spatial memory, which enables them to recognise their surroundings.

However, until recently it was believed that only humans possessed episodic memory – the ability to remember everyday experiences and events, which is associated with self-awareness – although any dog owner knows that the mere jangle of a lead or the sound of shoes being laced up can be enough to make a dog come to see if they are getting a walk.

In 2016, the first study of its kind on episodic memory in dogs was published in the journal *Current Biology*, led by animal psychologist Claudia Fugazza. It suggested that dogs may have more advanced memories than we thought. Dogs can't tell us about their experiences, so Fugazza designed an experiment that forced dogs to access their episodic memories.

First, a group of dogs was trained to perform six different actions by copying their owners. The owners then distracted the dogs from that expectation by having them lie down on a blue carpet after their owners performed the action, and only later gave the dogs the command to imitate. The memory retention intervals ranged from one minute to one hour: 'we found evidence that dogs can remember events as complex as human actions after incidental encoding … without motor practising the actions … This is the first evidence of episodic-like memory of others' actions in a non-human species, and it is the first report of this type of memory in dogs'.

IT'S ALL IN THE

Eyes

Dogs have large expressive eyes, which not only make them look cute, but the large pupils help them to see in low light conditions. Their field of vision is about 70 degrees wider than that of humans, but we have greater visual acuity and depth perception.

The design and performance of dog's eye is similar to a human's – it has a lens and a retina, the light sensitive area inside the eye, which is composed of two types of photoreceptors: cones and rods. Cones provide colour vision and high spatial acuity, but they require higher light levels, whereas the rods can provide vision at much lower light levels. It is a myth that dogs only see in black and white. They actually see in shades of yellow and blue, like a red-green colour-blind human.

A dog's eye has a higher ratio of rods to cones than a human's, so it only needs about one fifth of the light we need. It also has a special reflective layer behind the retina called the *tapetum lucidum*, which reflects light back onto the retina, improving low light vision even further (this is why a dog's eyes glow in the dark).

A dog's visual acuity is thought to be about 20/75, which means that if a dog could just read a car number plate from 20 feet away, a human with 20/20 vision could stand 75 feet away and still read it perfectly. However, acuity varies between dog breeds and it is thought that for example, Labradors, commonly used as seeing-eye dogs, may have vision that is closer to ours because they have been bred to have sharper eyesight.

Fortunately, dogs don't care much for reading number plates because they rely more on their smell and hearing and their eyes are still perfectly adapted to their canine needs, such as being able to hunt in the dim light of dawn and dusk. Alexandra Horowitz explains: 'when a dog turns his head toward you, it is not so much to look at you with his eyes; rather, it is to get his nose to look at you. The eyes just come along for the ride'.

Dogs don't have eyebrows – they don't need them, since eyebrows stop sweat from entering the eyes and dogs are covered in fur –

but their eyebrow area is still very expressive, and they often have markings above the eyes that accentuate the movements of the muscles to make the area more communicative.

Eye contact is an important part of canine communication and signals social hierarchy. Direct staring is used to establish dominance. When two dogs meet, the less dominant dog will avert his gaze, whilst the dominant dog maintains eye contact. Dogs also blink to appease and display friendly eye contact and to tell other dogs, 'I am friendly, I mean no harm'. Don't stare at strange dogs because they may perceive this as aggression. The best way to pacify an agitated dog is to minimise eye contact and, if you must approach it, talk in a soft voice with your body slightly angled, rather than square on.

> When two dogs meet, the less dominant dog will avert his gaze

A dog who avoids eye contact with humans has trust issues and is trying to steer clear of any kind of interaction, whether negative or positive. This dysfunctional behaviour is often seen in dogs that have been rescued from abusive situations. If these dogs are nurtured and made to feel safe, one of the major signs that they are on the road to recovery is when they are able to make eye contact again.

Despite the social dominance factor, it's OK to stare lovingly at your own dog, because he already knows and trusts you. If you want to blow kisses to your dog, gaze into his eyes and blink slowly to communicate trust, relaxation and calmness. In one study, scientists measured levels of the love hormone oxytocin in dogs and humans before and after locking eyes and reported a 130% increase in the dogs and a staggering 300% increase in the humans.

TELLTALE

Tails

We humans think we know what dogs do with their tails – wag for happy, tuck between the legs for sad and ambivalent in between. In fact, dogs use a much more subtle tail language that is always deliberate communication and never involuntary.

A dog will wag her tail at a bowl of food to express happiness and to thank her owner, but her tail wouldn't wag if she was alone. A dog's tail communicates its mental state, social position and intentions and doesn't have a mind of its own.

You may be surprised to learn that for the first three weeks of their lives, newborn puppies do not wag their tails because they don't need to, even though they are physically capable. The tail only becomes a necessary social communication tool when puppies start interacting with their littermates. By six or seven weeks of age, most puppies are regularly using their tails to signal their intentions and to avoid conflict. For example, you may have noticed that puppies wag their tails rapidly when they are suckling from their mother, not because they are ecstatically happy, but as an appeasement sign to the other puppies, as if to say, 'We may all be jostling for a teat, but this is feeding time, not rough and tumble, so let's all calm down, co-operate and tuck in'.

Tail language has three components – *position*, *shape* and – most importantly – *movement*, since this is effective over longer distances and because dogs' eyes can detect movement better than details or colours. Many dogs have lighter fur on the underside of their tails and highlights that make the tip more visible.

Tail position: Generally, when the tail is held high and maybe curls a little over the hind quarters, the dog is feeling confident and dominant. This also allows her scent to spread into the air to announce her presence. If she spots something interesting or catches an attention-grabbing smell, her tail may move to the horizontal, pointing away from her, but not stiff. She is now alert and attentive. If the tail then stiffens, such as when meeting another dog, it indicates possible conflict as they size each other up. If she then raises her tail up again, stiffly, she is communicating her dominance. She isn't being aggressive, just asserting herself. If the dog feels unsure or conflicted, the tail maintains a horizontal position. It will disappear between the hind legs during moments of high anxiety and fear or to signal subordination. This also covers up the scent glands and reduces the dog's olfactory presence – she literally takes up less smell space!

Tail shape: A dog's tail bristles as a sign of fear, anxiety or aggression, depending on the position of the tail. If the tail is held downwards, with bristling tip, this communicates fear and anxiety, but if a bristling tail is held high, and especially when accompanied by a crick (which might be subtle or very obvious, depending on the breed), this indicates a highly aggressive intent and is a very clear warning to back off.

Tail movement: Rapid tail wagging can convey excitement or tension, so you have to interpret the breadth of the wag and the speed to get the whole picture. Dogs wave their tails fast in a friendly broad sweep, often in a circular movement, when a member of the group returns or when something exciting is about to happen, like a walk. But tail wagging high, fast and stiffly can also be a sign of aggression and a submissive dog may wag its tail fast whilst cowering.

The direction of the wag is also significant. Dogs tend to wag more to the right when they meet a familiar person or dog and more to the left when meeting an unfamiliar person or dog or are facing possible conflict.

If you walk into a room and your dog is lying down, or you are both relaxing together and you give her a little stroke or say her name, she will often give you a single casual tail wag in return, simply to check in and remind you that she's contented and to acknowledge your importance in her life.

EXTRAORDINARY
Senses

Sighted humans see the world, dogs smell it. Dogs have 40 times more scent receptors than humans and the part of their brain that processes smell is much more sophisticated than ours. Alexandra Horowitz explains: 'The dog's universe is a stratum of complex odours. The world of scents is as least as rich as the world of sight … the dog is a creature of the nose'.

Smell is important for hunting prey but also for gathering information about other dogs. When dogs meet, they smell each other's faces, mouths, necks and hindquarters to exchange social-ranking information and a wealth of other data including mood, state of health, gender and fertility.

Dogs also have sweat glands between their toes that leave scent markers on the ground, to mark out their territory, so when your dog sniffs the ground he is picking up the smell of footprints left by other dogs.

Inside the human nose, the tissue has about 6 million sensory receptor sites; the inside of a dog's nose has up to 300 million and the olfactory bulbs in a dog's brain make up about one eighth of its entire mass. We can't begin to imagine the richness and complexity of smells that our dogs experience. Horowitz says, 'Dogs have more genes committed to coding olfactory cells, more cells and more *kinds* of cells, able to detect more kinds of smells. The difference in the smell experience is exponential', therefore a dog's sense of smell isn't simply 40 times more effective than our own, it may be millions of times more sensitive.

A dog's inconceivable sense of smell isn't limited to sensory receptors and the superior mass of dedicated brain space. In common with all snakes and lizards and many mammals, including cats, horses, cattle, pigs and some primates, dogs also possess an auxiliary olfactory sense called a vomeronasal organ (also known as Jacobson's organ). This is a specialised sac above the roof of the mouth along the nasal septum that is involved in a behaviour called the Flehmen response to detect pheromones and other complex animal scents. Humans have a vomeronasal organ, but it is vestigial.

To perform the Flehmen response, a cat or horse visibly curls back its upper lip to expose its front teeth, while dogs tend to lick the air, flick their tongues and smack their mouths and hold this position for several seconds. You might observe your dog doing this when you let him outside for the first time in the morning and he stands motionless with his head high, seeming to taste the air.

A dog's smell is so sensitive that it can detect how an odour has developed over time, which is what allows tracker dogs like bloodhounds to follow a scent and notice the difference between the same scent, in the same location, separated only by the passage of time (i.e. a dog could smell that two overlapping sets of footprints were made by the same person, several hours apart, enabling it to reconstruct the path that person has taken). It is also very likely that dogs can smell emotions such as fear, anxiety and anger because each is associated with a specific set of chemical signals.

Dogs are used by diabetics to detect when their blood sugar levels are dangerously high or low and they have also been able to accurately detect Parkinson's disease and certain types of cancer.

Steven Lindsay, a public health entomologist at Durham University in the UK, recently led research that proves dogs can be taught to detect malaria infection simply by smelling socks: 'Individuals that are infected with malaria parasites produce odours in their breath and from their skin that are specific signals'. Socks from 30 malaria-infected children and 145 uninfected children in the Gambia were frozen and sent to the UK where two dogs – a Labrador and a Labrador-retriever cross – were taught to distinguish which ones had been worn by infected children.

In light of the profound importance of smells in a dog's existence, Horowitz makes a philosophically fascinating observation about how they perceive us. She says, 'To dogs, we *are* our scent'.

EARS IN *Action*

Puppies are born deaf, and hearing is the last of the senses to fully develop. The ear canals begin to open after about ten days and the ears take about another ten days to function fully. When a dog's hearing is fully developed, he can hear four times the distance of a human with normal hearing.

Dogs have a hearing frequency range of 67Hz to 45,000Hz, which is very impressive relative to humans (64Hz to 23,000Hz), although this is a specious benchmark, because lots of animals have much better hearing than us. Horses outperform humans at both ends of the spectrum (55Hz to 33,500Hz), a cat's hearing is among the best in the animal kingdom (45Hz to 64,000Hz) and even the humble cow hears in the frequency range of 23Hz to 35,000Hz. In his book, *How Dogs Think*, Stanley Coren says, 'The truth of the matter is that, for some sounds, a dog's hearing is really hundreds of times better than ours, whereas for other sounds, dogs and humans have sound sensitivities that are very much the same'.

Hearing is a very important part of a dog's sensory world, as it is used to understand the intentions of other dogs, identify threats and locate prey (wolves prey on small rodents such as mice, so their survival depends on being able to hear their squeaks).

The internal anatomy of the ear is very similar, regardless of dog breed. For example, the ear canal travels at least two inches, even in small breeds, although as you would expect, the length and size of the canal varies in relation to overall body size. However, the external appearance varies greatly. Many breeds, from the Alaskan Malamute to the Chihuahua and the German Shepherd to the Welsh Corgi, have ears that are pointed and stand erect. Many others, from the Saint Bernard to the Cavalier and the Cocker Spaniel to the Golden Retriever, have ears that are floppy and droop down, and in the case of the Basset Hound – nearly touch the floor.

Dogs and humans first started co-existing sometime between 16,000 and 32,000 years ago. These dogs were essentially wolves, with pointy ears, dark fur, long muzzles and big jaws. Over thousands of years, humans selectively bred dogs with desirable traits such as tameness and friendliness and recent research has identified a resultant decrease of 'neural crest cells' in these tamer animals. These special cells, first identified by Swiss anatomist Wilhelm His Sr in 1868, help to shape a number of features of animal physiology, so that all domesticated animals, not just dogs, have smaller jaws and teeth, shorter snouts and tails, lighter fur or white fur patches and cuter more juvenile faces. Domestication has also produced significant changes to cartilage and connective tissues, hence the floppier ears.

Charles Darwin discussed ear shape in relation to the domestication of animals in *The Variation of Animals and Plants under Domestication*. He claimed that the elephant was the only wild animal with floppy ears and concluded, 'the incapacity to erect the ears is certainly in some manner the result of domestication'. He proposed that domesticated dogs had floppy ears because they no longer needed to be erect like funnels to catch every passing sound. He named the trend 'domestication syndrome'. As Darwin observed, the syndrome isn't unique to dogs – it appears in domesticated pigs, horses, sheep and rabbits. Hence, millennia of domestication have led to a cellular-level change in dogs, causing cute floppy ears.

There is no research proving that dogs with pointier ears are more aggressive and less friendly than those with floppier ears, but there is a public perception (or misconception) that floppy eared dogs are more approachable. For this reason, the Transportation Security Administration (TSA) – that oversees the security of the travelling public in the United States – currently recruits floppy-eared dogs to sniff out explosives. TSA Administrator David Pekoske explains: 'We've made a conscious effort in TSA … to use floppy ear dogs. We find the passenger acceptance of floppy ear dogs is just better. It presents just a little bit less of a concern. Doesn't scare children'.

A MEDLEY OF
BARKS

Wolves do not usually bark except when they are puppies and very excited, which suggests that thousands of years ago, the earliest dog owners must have deliberately bred their most vocal dogs together, so the resultant highly vocal animals would instinctively makes lots of noise whenever strangers approached their camp.

Puppies learn the basic canine signals if they are able to stay with their mothers and littermates for at least eight weeks. The basic rules involve three components: the *pitch* of a sound, its *duration* and its frequency or *repetition*. We recognise that dogs use a low-pitched sound, such as a growl, to indicate anger and threat. They use higher-pitched sounds such as yelps and squeals to express fear, pain or friendliness to appease other dogs and avoid a fight. This use of pitch isn't unique to dogs, it's common to many birds and mammals.

The second component – the duration of the sound – follows the general principle that the shorter sounds are associated with pain, fear or urgent need. According to Stanley Coren, author of *How to Speak Dog*, 'generally speaking, the longer the sound, the more likely that the dog is making a conscious decision about the nature of the signal and the behaviours that are about to follow'. So, the threatening growl of a dominant dog that means business and isn't bluffing, will be low-pitched but also 'long and sustained'. If a dog growls using shorter bursts that are less sustained, it's a sign that she is fearful and less confident of being able to win a fight.

The third component is the repetition rate of the sound. Coren explains: 'sounds that are repeated often, at a fast rate, indicate a degree of excitement and urgency. Sounds that are spaced out, or not repeated, usually indicate a lower level of excitement or a passing state of mind'.

Humans instinctively respond to these three components. For example, it is clear to us that if our dog stares out of the window and gives a couple of low-pitched perfunctory barks, her levels of excitement are much lower than if she were firing out multiple high-pitched bursts and repeating them. We are much more likely to respond to a fusillade of incessant barking than a few distracted woofs.

Coren states that all dogs express excitement in one or more of three ways, regardless of breed: 'the excitement whine, the moan-yodel ("Vowel-wowel-owel-wowel"), and the howl-yawn (a breathy "Hooooooo-ah-hooooo") … as the dog stares directly at you and twirls around to show its happy excitement'. Furthermore, his anecdotal research suggests that dogs that live together all use the same sound.

Here are a few different examples of barking which you will doubtless recognise if you're a dog owner:

Midrange pitch, rapid strings of three or four barks, with pauses in between: This means 'I think there's something out there; not sure what it is yet, but it's probably worth you taking a look'. If you respond to your dog and spend a short time investigating, your dog will quickly quieten down, job done.

Midrange pitch, rapid repeated barking: This means, 'High alert, action stations everyone, there is definitely someone at the door, or right outside'.

One or two short sharp barks, often accompanied by whines and squeals: This means, 'Hello, you're my friend. I love you. Welcome back!'

Prolonged string of barks with moderate to long intervals in between: This means, 'Is there anyone there? Where are you? I'm lonely folks, are you coming home soon? Please can you let me out of the kitchen now?'

Single short sharp bark: This is how a mother dog disciplines her puppies, but your dog may use it occasionally when she's overexcited and cheekily reprimands you for not giving her precisely what she wants right now! She may follow it up with a play bow because she knows she's being naughty!

FACIAL
EXPRESSIONS

Thousands of years of selective breeding have produced dogs with the ability to move their facial muscles in very subtle and sophisticated ways. They have integrated so well with humans that they interact with us using facial expressions. It's not just in our imaginations.

However, while dogs have some control over the upper part of their face, they have little voluntary control over the bottom half. In *How to Speak Dog*, Stanley Coren says, 'Dogs either don't have, or don't use, the voluntary neural control system to shape the expressions conveyed by their mouths'.

In various experiments, scientists have discovered that dogs are more facially expressive when they face their owners and that dogs produce more facial movements when a human is paying attention to them. So when your dog looks at you and raises his 'eyebrows' (especially his left one), this makes his eyes appear larger ('puppy eyes'), which makes him look cuter and communicates that he is happy to see you whilst also triggering your nurturing instincts.

Nevertheless, in a recent study led by Bridget Waller, professor of evolutionary psychology at the University of Portsmouth in the UK and published in the journal *Scientific Reports*, a video camera was used to record the facial movements of 24 dogs over a series of experiments. The results suggest that dog expressions per se are not merely an automatic response to internal emotions, but could be a mechanism of communication with humans, rather than 'something that is very emotionally driven and is very fixed'.

In *Inside of a Dog*, Alexandra Horowitz says, 'You can tell a lot about a dog by observing how he carries his head. Mood, interest and attention are writ in capital letters from the altitude of the head, the lay of the ears and the radiance of the eyes'. She gives as an example the 'clear, intentional gesture' of 'a dog prancing around in front of other dogs, tail and head high, with a cherished or stolen toy'.

Bowed head: Indicates that your dog is submissive. Even though this posture appears guilty, remember that dogs don't feel guilt, but they do apologise. A dog will lower his head and tail and may crouch down with his body to make it smaller and less threatening. Squinting during eye contact is also a sign of appeasement.

Head cocked to one side: Indicates uncertainty, or a sign that he is waiting for more information. Head cocking helps him pinpoint the direction of a sound and some experts believe it also helps him to see better, to compensate for the structure of the retina. Where humans have a little pit called a fovea, which provides the clearest vision, dogs with large muzzles have a line of high-density cells across the back of the retina called a 'visual streak'. Head cocking may compensate for a large muzzle, which blocks vision, as it is less prevalent in dogs with brachycephalic heads or flatter faces (these dogs tend to have a fovea, more like a human). Although the eyesight of these flat-faced dogs is less adapted for chasing things, they are better at reading human faces and emotions.

Frozen head: When your dog freezes his head or his whole body and leans forward, it is a sign that he is feeling threatened or challenged. Sometimes he will freeze and growl if you approach while he is chewing a toy. If this happens during play or a game of tug-of-war, your dog is being playful and preparing to whip his toy away from you to safety, otherwise you should give him some space.

Mouth closed and relaxed or opening slightly: Your dog is relaxed and happy.

Mouth closed and pulled back: Your dog is stressed, frightened, submissive or in pain.

Grimacing: When a dog's lips retract to show his teeth, usually accompanied by snarling and wrinkling of the muzzle, it is a warning to stay away. Remember, the key word, *warning*. The dog does not want to fight, but this is a very strong warning, which you should heed.

BODY
LANGUAGE

Dogs constantly use body language to communicate lots of important information about their emotional state, their status with respect to other dogs (and humans) and their intentions. The tail (see page 36) and ears (see page 42) warrant their own topics, so here is a general guide to help you understand what your dog's body is telling you.

But first, a quick reminder that dogs read your body language too, so it's important that your words match your actions. For example, if you want to stop your dog from doing something, saying 'No' with a firm voice and a gesture such as a frown or a downward wave of your arm is effective. Many people smile and cuddle their dogs at the same time, and might say in a sing song voice something like 'ooh, you are a naughty pup, aren't you?' This is a great way to confuse your dog and make her repeat the undesirable behaviour, thinking it's a game. Conversely, if she won't obey your recall command, your body language needs to remain happy and inviting, not telegraphing anger and frustration, which will make her stay well away.

Greeting: When two dogs meet, one of them may adopt a stiff-legged upright stance to express its dominance. If the other dog accepts this, she may break off eye contact and then lie down or perform a play bow to express submission. Once the social hierarchy has been quickly established, the dogs will proceed to sniff each other's faces, mouths and necks and finally hindquarters, whose scents give them even more social-ranking information. When two dogs of roughly equal status greet, they may both stand stiffly, flank to flank, as they sniff each other's hindquarters. If one of the dogs braces its feet and sticks its head forward with ears erect, it's a sign that the social hierarchy hasn't been established and that the dog is prepared to fight to assert its dominance.

Status: Another common display of dominance is when a dog places its head or paw on another dog, or shoulder barges it, or leans on the other dog, which is a less aggressive form of shoulder barge. Sometimes your dog will try to shoulder barge you out of the way when she wants to sit where you are. You're the boss, so hold your ground, even if you find the behaviour cute and hilarious.

Happy and relaxed: It is obvious when a dog is contented. The head is held in a neutral position, the mouth is relaxed, even hanging open slightly, tongue poking out a little so that you could swear she is actually smiling (this isn't as far-fetched as it sounds, because thousands of years of co-existence between dogs and humans, plus our tendency to anthropomorphise them, means that there is a evolutionary advantage for dogs whose facial expressions appear to mimic those of humans).

Playful: Dogs show each other that they are friendly and want to play by performing a play bow – but if excitement is really high, you may observe two dogs bound enthusiastically towards each other like two demolition drag racers going head to head, only to veer off at the final moment before they collide and perform the play bow. Or, if one dog is intimidated by the other, you might witness the dominant dog roll onto her back to encourage her timid companion to play.

Anxious and stressed: An anxious dog has many telltale signs. Its movement will be slow and hesitant, tail tucked beneath the legs, mouth closed and tight, ears pushed back against the head. Also, look out for excessive panting, licking of the lips and salivating. A dog may also raise her front paw when she is anxious, which is the first step of the procedure of rolling onto her back in full submission.

Angry and fearful: When anxiety turns to naked fear or anger, the dog's body expresses defensive aggression, the ears are pulled back tightly against the head, legs are stiff and locked on the threat, or she may stare into space, rather than maintain eye contact. Next comes body lunges forward and back, snarling and snapping, with lips drawn back and teeth bared. Even at this late stage, the dog's main motivation is to make the perceived threat go away rather than to unleash violence, which is the last resort.

DO DOGS NEED THEIR WHISKERS?

It is well known that cats gain a lot of useful sensory information from their whiskers and that they make an important contribution to how a cat navigates its surroundings. But what about your dog's whiskers? Some dogs only appear to have a handful and maybe a few straggly ones above the eyes.

The scientific name for whiskers – the stiff tactile hairs that grow out of an animal's face – is 'vibrissae'. Vibrissae differ from ordinary hair by being longer and thicker. The follicles are also larger and more deeply imbedded in the skin. They contain blood-filled sinus tissues and are surrounded by sensory nerves. Because of the principle of leverage, the slightest movement at the tip of one of these long whiskers is magnified as it is transmitted to the nerves at the other end, whether caused by brushing against an object or even by changes in airflow, which has been proved by recent studies with rats (scientists have known for a long time that rats use their whiskers to detect and localise airflow).

Depending on the breed, a casual inspection of your dog's face might make you think that he doesn't have very many whiskers, just a few stragglers sticking out of his muzzle, but you will discover more if you look more closely. Superciliary/supraorbital vibrissae grow above the eyes, chin vibrissae on the chin, mandibular vibrissae below the jaw and a small clump of zygomatic/genal vibrissae grow out of the cheeks.

The clearly visible whiskers that grow in rows on either side of his muzzle are called 'mystacial vibrissae' and they are commonly found on many mammals from rats to bears and seals.

Some dog breeders and groomers cut off these whiskers to give the head a 'cleaner' look for dog shows. In fact, some show breeds, such as poodles, are penalised for having whiskers.

Be in no doubt that you should never cut your dog's whiskers, even if you think they look messy or asymmetrical. In common with cats and other mammals, whiskers complement a dog's sense of sight and they are especially important in low light conditions or when the animal has trouble seeing something close by. They also help your dog measure the size of the space he is in. If you gently touch or even go near one of your dog's supraorbital vibrissae you will notice that he closes his eyes. These whiskers clearly provide protection for his eyes, so that your dog gets warning about something that could hurt his eyes a nanosecond before possible impact, in the same way that humans who are blind or visually impaired might use a cane to detect objects in their path.

Groomers and competitive dog showers would no doubt argue that modern dogs don't rely on whiskers the way their wild cousins, wolves, do and therefore they do not suffer for the loss, especially because whiskers can grow back. However, scientists have located corresponding areas in the somatosensory cortex area of a dog's brain that process the information gained by whiskers, proving that they are important for dogs and by no means vestigial. Even hairless breeds of dogs and cats usually still have whiskers.

Stanley Coren argues, 'Amputating vibrissae is both uncomfortable and stressful for dogs … dogs whose vibrissae have been removed seem more uncertain in dim light … With intact vibrissae, the dog actually does not have to make physical contact with a surface to know it is there'.

According to dog trainer and animal behaviour consultant Liz Palika, whiskers can also communicate a dog's emotional state: 'A dog or cat at rest will have his whiskers in a relaxed neutral position. When afraid, the whiskers tend to sweep back, sometimes to the point of being close to the cheeks. When angry, hunting, or alert, the whiskers will stand out or sweep forward'. This means that your dog's whiskers may even be important for communicating with other dogs.

UNIQUE COMMUNICATION BETWEEN YOU AND

Your Dog

The previous section dealt mainly with how dogs use body language to communicate with other dogs, but they also use facial expressions and body signals to connect with humans and express their needs, moods and often just to tell us that they love us.

Eye contact: As already discussed on page 35, eye contact is an important part of canine communication and also signals social hierarchy. Your dog stares at you with soft eyes because he knows and trusts you but also because that is a way to ask for something, so pay attention. If you are sitting at your computer or watching television and your dog comes into the room and stares at you, he may be asking to be fed or he could be asking to be let outside. He might be silently reminding you that it's long past his walk time. Late in the evening, he may be begging for you to go to bed, so that he can also get some uninterrupted sleep. At these moments, most of us naturally find ourselves talking to our dogs and asking them what they want. In fact, if you ask 'What do you want?' followed by 'Show me' and then stand up and follow your dog, you can actually teach him that 'Show me' is a sign that you are being super attentive and are trying to understand what he wants. Some intelligent dogs will learn that this is their cue to walk to the door, or to have you follow them into the kitchen where an empty water bowl needs filling.

Flapping his ears: The occasional flappy-eared shake of the head is perfectly normal, but if your dog keeps doing it, or paws at his ear, it could be a sign of an ear infection, or irritants such as a grass seed, ear mites or an insect, especially if he's recently been playing around in water. Don't ignore it. Speak to your vet.

Licking you: There are lots of reasons why dogs lick our bare skin. Sometimes they can be quite enthusiastic and at other times they seem to do it almost out of a sense of duty. Dogs may lick because they like the salty taste of their owner's skin, as a sign of affection, or because they are bored. But they mostly just enjoy doing it and find it soothing. If a puppy licks the side of your mouth, he could be trying to make you sick up your breakfast: 'Researchers of wild canids … report that puppies lick the face and muzzle of their mother when she returns from a hunt to her den in order to get her to regurgitate for them', notes Alexandra Horowitz in her book, *Inside Of A Dog.*

Sitting on your feet or between your legs: This is often mistaken for possessive behaviour but is usually a sign of anxiety or nervousness. When dominance appears to be the problem, think fear instead. Your dog is trying to feel safer by sticking close to you.

Tongue flicking: If there is no food present and your dog tongue flicks and licks his lips, it's a sign of anxiety and if it persists it could be a sign that he's in pain. Dogs also tongue flick when they want to appease or avoid conflict.

Yawning: On page 64, mirroring is mentioned as a sign of love. If your dog yawns directly after you, it's a strong sign that he empathises with you. However, if he yawns a few times on his own or sneezes, he is feeling uncertain and uncomfortable. Look around for the cause. It could be a strange person or dog, or because you are acting strangely, or rustling a plastic bag, or maybe you startled him by noisily ripping off a length of aluminium foil in the kitchen. There's always a reason if you look hard enough.

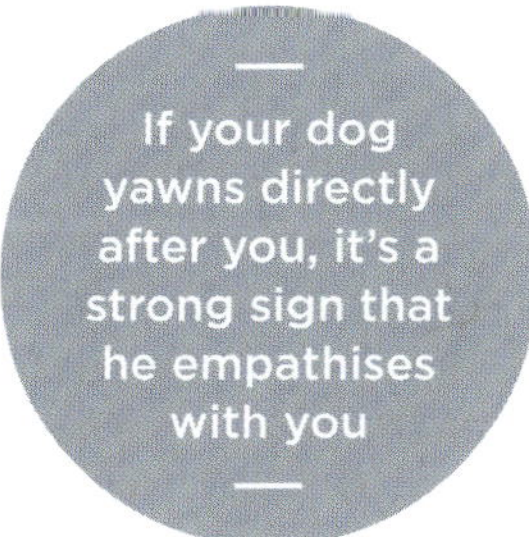

JUMPING

Up

It is common for dogs, especially puppies, to jump up on you with their front paws when you get home. They want to get near your face, so they can get in a good sniff and a lick, like canids in the wild do when a pack member returns.

Some owners argue that if it doesn't bother anyone, then it's no big deal, but there are lots of good reasons for discouraging it. If the dog is little, she will scrabble around below the level of your knees, which is bad enough because she could easily get trodden on and injured. A big dog jumping up could easily knock over a child, a frail person or get muddy paw prints all over someone's clothes. If you are still prepared to take the risk, then that is to ignore the responsibility as a dog owner to show some courtesy. Why should other people have to tolerate your dog's unwanted behaviour?

Jumping up is so easily fixed, that if a dog household tolerates this, you can bet the dog is getting away with lots of other bad behaviour as well. In fact, this same laziness/reluctance to show leadership by owners can spread into all aspects of dog management. A dog that jumps up probably misbehaves and pulls when she's on a lead, barks excessively, digs holes in the garden, chews sticks, destroys the furniture, begs for food at every meal … the list is endless. Jumping up is the thin end of a badly chewed wedge. If you can't be bothered to fix that, what hope have you got of giving your dog the proper guidance and boundaries that she needs? Training your dog to behave doesn't make you a control freak, it makes you a kind and responsible owner.

Some experts advise you to firmly place your dog's front paws on the ground, say 'down' and then ignore her until she's calm, but it's more effective to take away your attention completely. Come in through the door and if your dog jumps up, turn your back and busy yourself with something else. Don't acknowledge the behaviour, don't say 'no' or 'down', simply remove the very thing that your dog wants – your attention. As soon as the dog calms down, then you can give her lots of praise and fuss. If you ignore a jumping dog, she will quickly learn that only dogs with four feet on the ground get praise and attention. Consistency is vital when it comes to any rules of the house. Make sure everyone in the household is consistent, otherwise your dog will get anxious and confused.

Some dog owners have the problem of their dog jumping up and even playfully biting them repeatedly during a walk. There are several possible reasons for this, so it's important to treat each case individually. However, there will be common features, such as overexcitement and excess energy, plus the reaction of the owner will in some way be reinforcing the behaviour (otherwise it would stop). If you have tried ignoring, but find it impossible because the dog keeps jumping up and biting you or grabbing your clothes, then the first thing you need to do is to exercise your dog more frequently. It is clear that your dog has too much nervous energy, plus you have probably reduced the number of walks because her behaviour is so frustrating.

Follow through completely with your strategy. If this means ignoring her, then do it for longer. Stand still, say nothing, do nothing. If this really is impossible then attach your dog's leash to a tree and walk away a few paces (so she can see you haven't abandoned her completely), then turn your back and ignore her until she calms down. When she is calm, return and give her praise. If that winds her up again so that she starts jumping and biting, walk away again. Be consistent and persistent. This could take several days or even weeks to reprogram.

CLUES YOUR DOG

Loves You

When your dog stares at you with his tail wagging, eyes shining and his mouth lolling open, tongue hanging languidly out of one side, and you swear he is actually smiling at you, make no mistake, your dog loves having you around. But dogs also have more subtle ways of expressing their love.

As you stare into each other's eyes, the posterior lobe of the pituitary gland – a pea-sized structure at the base of both of your brains – secretes the love hormone oxytocin, which makes you feel good and deepens your mutual bond. At the same time, his ears may be facing forward and alert, to indicate that he is listening to you, or one or both ears may be pinned flat against his head in a gesture of submission. If he is happy, this expresses trust rather than anxiety.

Sometimes dogs lean against each other to show dominance, but if your dog leans against you, it may be a sign that he is feeling anxious and is seeking your reassurance, or in other circumstances it can be a protective gesture, to let those around know that he loves you and wants to protect you.

Mirroring is another sign of love. If your dog yawns directly after you, it's a strong sign that he empathises closely with you. In fact, studies have shown that dogs will copy an owner's behaviour as long as ten minutes afterwards. 'Researchers have known that human beings prefer the behaviour of other people who subtly imitate their gestures and other affects', says Duane Alexander, director of the Eunice Kennedy Shriver National Institute of Child and Human Development, so humans have unwittingly bred dogs to do this. In fact, research has found that dogs will automatically imitate humans, even when it is not in their best interest to do so. A recent study published in the *Proceedings of the Royal Society B* showed that ten dogs of various breeds were inclined to copy their owners, even if it meant forsaking a food reward.

According to neuroscientist Dr Gregory Berns, author of *How Dogs Love Us*, if your dog wants a cuddle after eating, that's significant. Food is a dog's highest priority in life, but Berns says that once your dog has wolfed his dinner, what he does directly afterwards will indicate what is most important to him besides eating. So, if he chooses a post-prandial snuggle with you, it is a clear sign that your dog really loves and values you.

Many dog experts claim that dogs hate being hugged, but many dogs enjoy physical contact; they like curling up against or on you, they enjoy you lying next to them on the floor or on a bed. Many dogs seek out physical affection and will allow you to nuzzle your face gently against theirs, but most will struggle to escape if you give them a tight bear hug, so be sensitive to your dog's body language and don't force affection on him against his will.

—

Many dog experts claim that dogs hate being hugged

—

If your dog steals your clothes, it's another subtle sign that he loves you and the smell of you (which is on your clothes). Sniffing your familiar scent on your clothing or dragging items back to his bed so that he can snuggle with them, makes him feel safe and secure.

If your dog brings you gifts, such as his favourite toys, it doesn't necessarily mean he wants to play – he could just be telling you that he loves you by presenting you with one of his most treasured possessions (see page 67).

If your dog remains calm when you leave the house (even if those big brown eyes appear sad), it is a very healthy sign that he trusts you to return soon. If he gets very agitated before you leave and is destructive while you are away, this is a sign of major anxiety (see page 71). When you return, his excitement is another obvious indication that he's crazy about you.

THE JOY OF
GIVING

Many breeds of dog love nothing better than to bring you stuff – sometimes lots of it. It is very common for a Golden Retriever to greet you when you get home, and then rush off to bring you one of its toys – which is very cute. Gift giving is a completely normal behaviour for dogs and many breeds do it.

When your dog brings you one of her toys, this is a healthy sign that she sees you as her Alpha. The act of giving sends many signals. It is a gesture of respect, submission and trust. It is a demonstration that your dog is delighted to see you. It's also a result of your dog having lots of energy, because if you've been away for a while, there's a good chance she's spent most of that time asleep.

Gift giving also ensures that you give your dog your full attention and it is often an invitation to play. Some dogs will try to put the object into your hand to initiate a game, such as tug-of-war. It's not always convenient for you to drop everything and rough play with your dog every time you return home, but you should accept many of your dog's invitations because this builds trust and also gives your dog the satisfaction of knowing that her efforts to communicate have been successful.

Receiving a gift doesn't always have to mean that it's play time, but it's very important to acknowledge your dog after you have been away by at the very least accepting her gift and giving her some attention, since she's been alone in an empty house for several hours.

If you find her innocent bid for attention an annoyance, this doesn't mean your dog is at fault. It's a hard heart that can treat such blithe enthusiasm with indifference or annoyance, no matter how hard your day has been. You are the Alpha and the dog should not rule the house, but she is part of your household and as a dog owner you have a responsibility to understand your dog's emotional needs and to build her self-esteem. If, however, your dog proudly drags over a limited edition Christian Louboutin velour trainer – you have a problem.

In this situation, don't shout at the dog. Stay calm. You have two choices. You can either ignore her until she loses interest in the trainer, and then rescue it when her attention is elsewhere, or if you can't bear to see your beloved footwear suffer for another second, give her a firm command: 'No, drop it'. This will only work if you've already trained your dog to drop. If she drops it, praise her immediately. If she doesn't, you will probably have to fetch an edible treat to bribe her with. This is OK. You aren't teaching her that she will get a reward every time she destroys your stuff – in future she won't have the opportunity, because you will lock away your precious belongings where your naturally curious dog can't find them. It's really that simple. Remove the opportunity and the crisis goes away. Your dog is not the problem.

The same goes for objects that could harm her. For example, Labradors are renowned for eating socks, which often leads to an anxious trip to the vets for a scan and even a life-saving operation. If your dog can get access to your treasured stuff, then there's a good chance that your lifestyle choices (i.e. your pathological inability to tidy things away) are putting her in danger. So, take the chewed remains of your box-fresh Nike Air Jordans as a wake-up call rather than a reason to punish.

Make sure your dog has access to plenty of safe chew toys because chewing is a natural and necessary activity for a dog and especially for a teething puppy. Notice which toys your dog prefers and make sure you rotate them regularly so she doesn't get bored.

WHY SO *Needy?*

If your dog follows you everywhere around the house and always wants to be with you, you have what some people call a 'Velcro dog'. This isn't necessarily a bad thing, if you are happy with the constant attention and your dog is contented and healthy, well exercised and stimulated.

A dog who always wants to be by your side is only a problem if either you or the dog are unhappy with the situation. Certain breeds, such as lap dogs or working, herding and hound dogs that work alongside their owners all day, are more likely to form such strong attachments because they have been bred to be more dependent and they look to humans for guidance and management.

On dog owner forums you'll find strict training advice such as 'don't overdo the love' or 'show you're the boss' or 'if you are strong and confident, your dogs will be too, as a reflection of you'. There's some truth to all of that, but it isn't the whole picture and these statements on their own are too reductive and won't fix the problem, if you decide there's a problem to fix.

There are several scenarios in which over attachment is unhealthy and needs to be addressed:

Your dog is the Alpha: If you don't firmly but kindly establish yourself as the Alpha in your family, your dog will reluctantly assume the mantle, which makes most dogs anxious because it's a huge responsibility to protect everyone and keep them safe, especially when you leave the house, because he frets the whole time you're away.

Boredom: If your dog isn't getting enough exercise and mental stimulation, he may become clingy and make you the central source of entertainment, especially if it gets him lots of attention. For example, if your dog follows you into the bathroom, he may have learned that he gets lots of petting while you are sitting on the toilet. If he gets over-excited the moment you get off the couch, it's a sign that he's not getting enough exercise and may even be anticipating the moment that you put your shoes on to fetch the dog lead.

Neglect: Some dogs become clingy after being left on their own too much. A secure and happy dog will stay calm when you leave the house. If your dog gets highly anxious before you leave, he may have separation anxiety.

Separation anxiety: The most common symptoms are: barking or howling when you've gone, causing damage, defecating or urinating while you're away, pacing, excessive panting or drooling (a sign of high anxiety) and becoming anxious when anyone prepares to leave the house. Unless your dog has been badly neglected in the past, this is fixable by reducing the amount of time you leave your dog alone and by offering something like a Kong toy filled with healthy treats to keep him entertained. Talk to your vet for further advice.

Vision or hearing problems: If your dog develops hearing or vision loss, he may seek comfort by sticking by your side. This will usually present gradually over several months or years, but if your dog exhibits a sudden change of behaviour, clings to you and shows signs of anxiety or lethargy, consult your vet because this may be a sign of an illness.

Moving house: Moving house is stressful for dogs as well as humans. Your dog will have to learn all about his new environment, and anxious dogs may find it stressful to explore the strange territory. During this time, you are the only familiar part of his world. You can help him to settle in by establishing a predictable routine with plenty of exercise in his new surroundings.

If you want to address your dog's neediness, talk to your vet for advice and read some specialist books on the subject such as: *It's Okay to be Alone: a Hands-on Guide to Coping with Separation Anxiety* by Julie Hindle or *Be Right Back!: How To Overcome Your Dog's Separation Anxiety and Regain Your Freedom* by Julie Naismith.

A FASCINATION WITH

Most dogs love to gather and chew sticks, and it can be very entertaining to watch your dog struggling to drag home a huge branch that she can hardly carry, let alone navigate through your front gate. Dogs are naturally curious and they love to explore their surroundings.

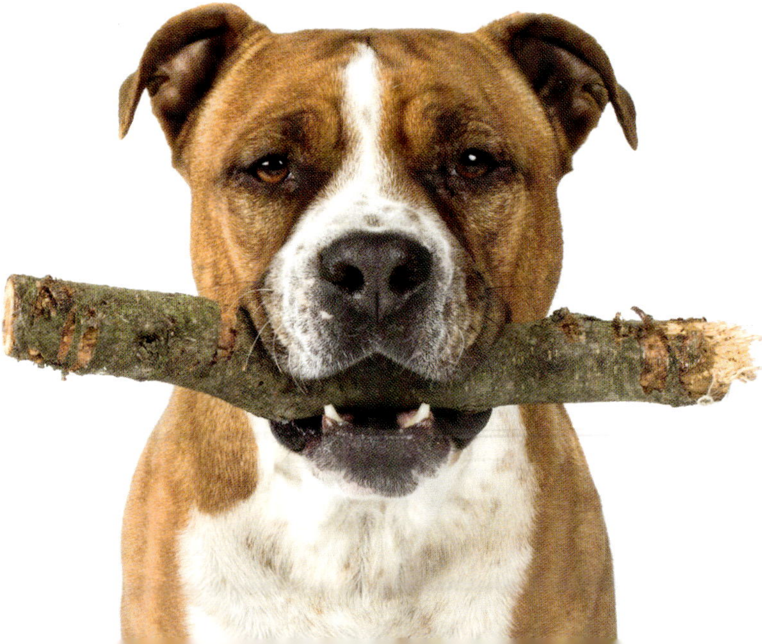

Some of the appeal of a stick may have something to do with its superficial similarity to a bone, which would be your dog's main source of food if she was living in the wild. But dogs aren't so easily fooled. They are intelligent animals with highly developed senses and they are guided more by their noses and hearing than by eyesight.

Their predator instinct tells them to chew to reach the tasty marrow, but a stick doesn't smell anything like a juicy bone, so there must be more going on. A stick does have a unique earthy, woody odour and a crunchy texture that makes it attractive to smell and chew, even when it turns out not to be a juicy bone. Also, some breeds, such as gun dogs, are trained to recover birds and other items, so they have a genetic preference for finding objects and then carrying them in their mouths.

> Their predator instinct tells them to chew to reach the tasty marrow

Dogs enjoy sourcing their own toys and foraging for sticks, which also satisfies their urge to search and hunt. But chewing is also an important way that dogs explore the world. 'Chewing, for a dog, is like a human opening a door and looking into a room', explains Colin Tennant, chairman of the UK Canine and Feline Behaviour Association: 'People are nosy, and so are the dogs. But they investigate with their mouths, because they don't have hands'.

For young dogs chewing can provide temporary relief from the pain of erupting teeth, but all dogs chew to keep their jaws strong and teeth clean. It's also a good way to alleviate boredom or to reduce anxiety. If your back garden is littered with chewed sticks, you might want to offer your dog a wider range of toys and make sure that she is getting sufficient exercise.

A major downside of chewing sticks is that when swallowed, splinters can cause serious internal injury that can only be fixed by emergency surgery. But even if your dog doesn't swallow, splinters can get caught between teeth and damage gums and cheeks and even puncture her palate. An old rotten stick will crumble harmlessly, but newer wood can be more dangerous, so you need to stay vigilant, or discourage your dog from chewing sticks altogether. Keep sacks of shop bought domestic kindling away from your dog as it splinters very easily. Also, make an inventory of the trees and shrubs in your garden and on her walks, so that your dog doesn't chew something poisonous such as Walnut, Red Maple, Black Cherry or Yew, to name just a few.

If you decide that the risk of injury is too great, you can discourage your dog's interest in sticks by using positive reinforcement, by encouraging her to play with safe chew toys (you'll find a large, if rather pricey, selection in your local dog care store) or a tennis ball and by refusing to engage with her when she picks up a stick and wants to play, or by removing the stick and distracting her with another more fun activity. It is better to say 'Leave it' and then reward her with a food treat when she obeys, than to allow her to pick up the stick and then get rewarded for dropping it.

—

You can discourage your dog's interest in sticks by using positive reinforcement

—

But even if she learns that she can get your attention by picking up a stick, at least she won't have the opportunity to injure herself by chewing it. Also, stick collecting can become a timely warning that your dog wants more stimulation.

TO SLEEP, PERCHANCE
to Dream

Dogs sleep more than humans and it can even be said that they are expert catnappers, but how can we be sure that they dream? They certainly look like they are chasing rabbits in their sleep when their legs twitch and pedal whilst they utter a string of muted barks.

Scientists have been studying dog sleep for decades and they have discovered that not only do dogs dream, but that their sleep patterns phase through similar periods of wakefulness, rapid-eye-movement (REM) sleep and non-rapid-eye-movement sleep, to those of humans. These same sleep phases have been detected in many animals, using an electroencephalogram to measure brain wave activity.

Dogs spend just over half their time drowsily resting or sleeping. During a study published in *Physiological Behaviour* in 1977, six pointer dogs had their brain waves measured for 24 hours. They spent 44% of their time alert, 21% drowsy, 12% in REM sleep and the remaining 23% in the deepest stage of non-REM sleep, called slow-wave sleep.

Sleep is important for your dog's mental and physical health and plays a key role in consolidating memory, helping to sift through the events of the day and determining what passes into long-term memory. Dogs enter the REM state about 20 minutes after falling asleep and might spend two or three minutes there. The breath becomes irregular, their eyes will start to move around more rapidly, eyelids flickering, and limb muscles might twitch, especially with puppies and elderly dogs, for whom limb paralysis is less effective during sleep. Scientists also believe that smaller dogs have more frequent but shorter dreams while large dogs have less frequent but longer dreams.

'Dogs do dream,' confirms psychology professor Stanley Coren, author of *Do Dogs Dream? Nearly Everything Your Dog Wants You to Know*. We would expect this because the similarity in brain patterns indicates that dogs probably dream in a similar way to humans: reliving their daily experiences and enacting waking activities. But scientists have performed experiments in which they have managed to disable the part of the brain that causes the temporary paralysis that prevents animals from coming to harm by acting out their dreams. This band of nerve fibres in the brain stem is called the *pons*. Scientists have deactivated the pons and then, under controlled conditions, observed dogs acting out their dreams in breed-specific activities. 'What we've basically found is that dogs dream doggy things,' explains Coren. 'A sleeping Springer Spaniel may flush an imaginary bird in its dreams, while a dreaming Doberman Pinscher may pick a fight with a dream burglar'.

Coren also provides anecdotal evidence in the form of a letter he received 'which seems to confirm the idea of dogs having dreams about their everyday activities'. In the letter, a dog owner called Joseph Baker reported that his dog – a Basenji named Goober – ran under his legs after having a bad dream, copying a waking behaviour that the dog only ever performed after having a bath. This led Joseph to conclude that Goober had dreamed about his dreaded bath time.

If your dog is whining, crying or growling, he may be having a bad dream in which he feels threatened or anxious. If he's a particularly lively dreamer, you may start to worry that his twitching muscles and paddling feet are the symptoms of a seizure, but so long as the rest of the body is relaxed, you can be reassured that he is just acting out his dreams. During a seizure, the body movements are more noticeably violent; the whole body goes rigid and twitches in unison, racked by powerful electrical shocks as the synapses in the brain repeatedly misfire. The back arches, the dog may foam at the mouth and wet himself. After waking from a seizure, the dog will pace around in an agitated state, panting for up to an hour.

If you want to wake your dog from a nightmare, quietly call his name using a reassuring tone, but don't try to rouse him physically. After all, it's just a bad dream and he'll soon wake up without your help.

TEARING UP THE RULES AND OTHER PROBLEM

BeHAViouR

Problem behaviour should be defined as any conduct that disturbs the harmony and wellbeing in your household or causes conflict and distress outside the home while you are in public with your dog. These actions might be destructive, anti-social, unhygienic, unhealthy, dangerous or a combination of all these things.

First, when talking about 'problem behaviour', it doesn't simply apply to your dog. Whether you see her as a member of the family or find the idea too sentimental, it is a simple fact that your dog is a social animal. Like it or not, your dog is part of your family and she sees herself in these terms. She looks to you for training and guidance and it's your duty as leader to help her become a valued and loved member of the team.

Whether you take a puppy into your home from a breeder or adopt an adult dog from an animal shelter with a documented history of abuse and some inevitable problem behaviours, you accept the responsibility to give that animal the resources she needs to integrate into your family and to lead a safe, fulfilling and meaningful life. Neuroscientist Dr Gregory Berns, author of *How Dogs Love Us*, perfectly sums up the challenge of this role: 'To truly live with dogs, humans need to become "great leaders". Not dictators who rule by doling out treats and by threatening punishment, but leaders who respect and value their dogs as sentient beings'.

Berns believes that the most important characteristics of a great leader are 'clarity and consistency' and he also issues a warning: 'while it is easy to confuse being a pack leader with being dominant, that is a mistake that has harmed more dogs than any other piece of advice'.

Are you starting to see the picture? If your dog is displaying 'problem behaviour', you have to take a holistic approach and view it in its wider context, by examining the triggers and the household dynamics that might be contributing to her actions. 'Behavioural problems often stem from a lack of clear inter-species communication', says Adrienne Farricelli, author of *Brain Training for Dogs*, 'and all that is needed is to better understand what our dogs are trying to say'.

For example, sometimes we send the wrong signals and reinforce the behaviour we want to avoid, such as picking up a dog or petting them when they are growling or barking at a visitor or at another dog. Neither should you punish the dog. Both approaches will reinforce the undesired behaviour. Your instinctive reaction should always be to try to understand what your dog is trying to tell you rather than to punish, so that you can solve the puzzle.

First of all, growling is a sign that the dog doesn't want to use violence. It is a warning explicitly intended to avoid conflict that means, 'back off, I don't want to fight you'. Sadly, we all too often interpret it as meaning the exact opposite. You don't want to discourage your dog's ability to communicate by growling, because otherwise she may end up biting without being able to issue a warning. If you punish your dog for growling, all you are teaching her is that the next time she'll have to escalate the situation immediately in order to be understood.

The Association of Professional Dog Trainers offers succinct advice about treating aggression: 'Dogs that use aggression to "get what they want" are not displaying dominance, but rather anxiety-based behaviours, which will only increase if they are faced with verbal and/or physical threats from their human owners'. The American Society for the Prevention of Cruelty to Animals (ASPCA) also unambiguously denounces old-school dominance training: 'Techniques like alpha rolls, scruff shakes and other violent manoeuvres frighten many dogs and can trigger defensive aggression … They're also irrelevant to most behaviour problems, and they can erode the bond between dog and pet parent'.

Dogs, like children, learn best by positive reinforcement, a simple technique that rewards desired ('good') behaviour and ignores undesirable ('bad') behaviour. See page 25 for a more detailed explanation.

EMBARRASSING CANINE

Dogs are a beguiling mixture of qualities, but not only are their crazier quirks a major inconvenience, they can leave us feeling embarrassed and grossed out. How can such noble and cute animals, our best friends, also make us so uncomfortable?

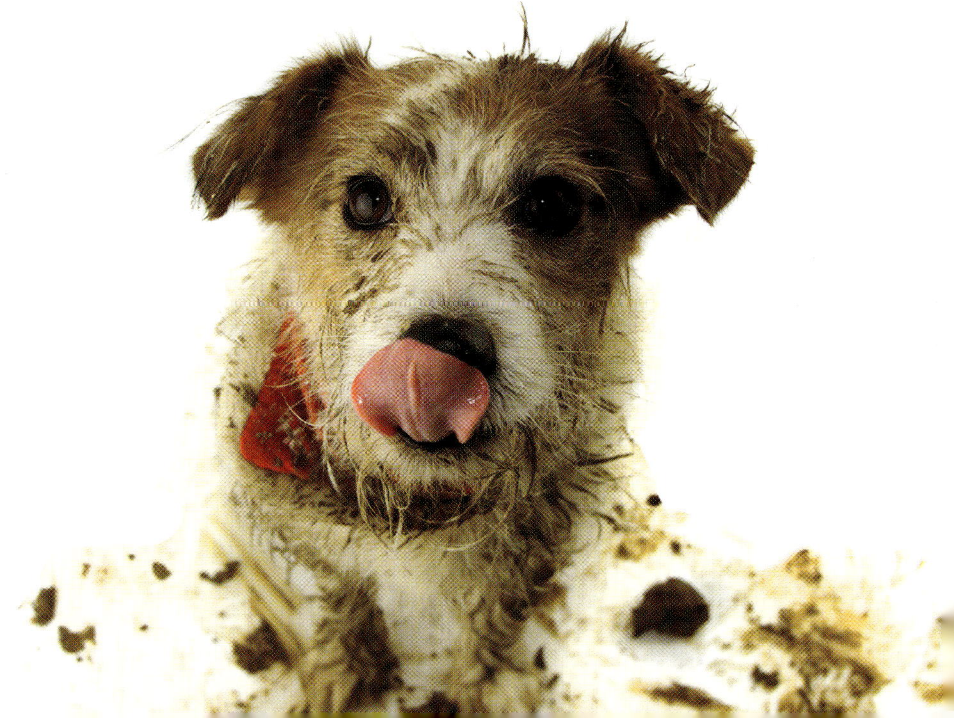

Even though some of these behaviours seem strange to humans, they can be quite normal for dogs. It helps to understand the reasons why dogs develop so many seemingly bizarre habits, because there is a sound explanation for every one of them – and sometimes it's your fault.

Sniffing crotches and backsides: Dogs learn a lot of important information about each other by sniffing each other's hindquarters, including gender and social standing, mood, state of health and fertility. So, when a human comes into your house, it is natural for them to hone in on the area where they can gain lots of scent data, although it's usually only the bigger dogs who have the height to reach. It just takes a few seconds and then the dog should move onto other things.

Rolling in faeces and dead animals: Dogs love to find a big fresh pile of horse or stinky fox or badger droppings and rub the sides of their faces and their flanks with it. When they're at the beach, a dead fish or seagull can hold a similar attraction. This behaviour is very widespread within the animal kingdom. Biologists have studied scent rubbing in captive wolves by providing them with a range of different odours, with surprising results. The wolves show least interest in the faeces of their prey and were most attracted to artificial odours like perfume or motor oil and also the scent of other predators, such as cougars and black bears. Scent rolling is now believed to offer protection against predators rather than fool an animal's own prey. This theory has been further supported by the filming of grey foxes scent marking in the urine of mountain lions to ward off other large predators like coyotes.

Eating faeces: The only 'normal' circumstances for eating faeces are when dogs are experimenting as puppies or when a mother dog cleans up after her puppies. Otherwise, it warrants further investigation. It can be a symptom of certain medical conditions like diabetes, hyperthyroidism or intestinal parasites that increase appetite, or it could be a way to compensate for nutritional deficiencies such as digestive enzymes. Some experts label it as a psychological condition caused by over-strict house-training. Other reasons include attention-seeking, boredom and stress.

Drinking from the toilet or licking the bowl: Dogs love to drink fresh, preferably running, water that is cool and well oxygenated. If the water in your dog's bowl is stale and unappealing, he may go in search of cool refreshment by drinking from the toilet. Unfortunately, this water is also teeming with bacteria and chemicals such as bleach, so keep the bathroom door closed and place several water bowls around the house (ceramic or metal, not plastic), change them several times a day and wash them every evening in warm soapy water.

Jumping up on people: Dogs jump up to greet humans because they want to sniff our faces, like they do when greeting dogs. If you want to stop it, simply ignore your dog when he jumps up and only give him praise and attention when he comes back down to earth.

Scooting across the floor on his backside: Your dog has an itchy backside caused by impacted anal sacs (which should really be emptied by a vet rather than onto your carpet), which could be caused by worms, an allergy or injury.

Humping furniture or someone's leg: This is most likely to be a display of social dominance as dogs – especially adolescents – mount other dogs to dominate them. But it can also occur simply because your dog is overexcited and/or attention-seeking at the arrival of visitors. Don't make a big deal out of it. Just push the dog down firmly, rather than punish or scold and then give him praise and attention when he has calmed down.

STRESS, ANXIETY AND
Depression

Until fairly recently, many scientists have been reluctant to countenance the idea that dogs might have an emotional life similar to humans, even with respect to their ability to feel pain. Fortunately, there is now a consensus that dogs experience stress and anxiety and that they can and do suffer from depression.

Although some dogs are born with a predisposition to anxiety and fearfulness, in most cases this is caused by the immediate environment and can also be linked to negative experiences or incomplete socialisation during a puppy's formative early months.

If you get your dog from a breeder, you would expect to take her home when she is eight weeks old. You then have a narrow window of about six weeks in which to expose your puppy to a variety of situations, people and experiences. Of course, this process of socialisation continues over the first 12 months, but these early weeks, when your puppy is fearless and curious, are crucial.

You shouldn't walk your puppy in public until she has had her second set of vaccinations, at around 11-12 weeks old, but this mustn't stop you from carrying her on lots of trips around your area so she is exposed to lots of different people, places and other dogs, so long as they have had their vaccinations.

This busy period of socialisation can calm down after your puppy has reached 18 weeks of age, but negative experiences can implant readily during the first year. If she gets anxious in certain situations or freaks out every time she sees a German Shepherd or men with beards, for example, don't shield her from these things by avoiding them – do the exact opposite, give her greater exposure and turn these meetings into happy experiences full of treats and fun, so that she begins to see these things as normal. She will take her cues from you and so for the first year of her life it's paramount that you stay calm and teach her that the world is a fun and safe place with lots to explore.

If your dog has already developed a fear or phobia, this will be because of a negative experience some time in her puppyhood that wasn't resolved at the time. Unfortunately, giving your dog lots of attention, attempting to soothe her and calling her a good girl when she is expressing fear, only draws attention to the feared thing and reinforces the phobia. Consult your vet, who will advise you on desensitisation techniques and may offer medications to relieve distress.

Depression in dogs is linked to the same chemical deficiencies in the brain as in humans, including a lack of the neurotransmitter serotonin. Environmental conditions such as bereavement or separation, moving house, a new baby or pet, trauma from illness, injury or abuse such as violence or long periods of isolation, can all cause depression in dogs. The two most common triggers are the loss of an owner or companion animal.

There are nine million dogs in the UK alone, and a recent report by a pet insurance company indicated that anxiety and depression are widespread among domestic pets, with 623,000 dogs and cats in the UK suffering mentally each year and more than 900,000 suffering a loss of appetite because of stress or emotional problems.

Dog depression symptoms are very similar to those in people. A depressed dog will become withdrawn, inactive, lose interest in walks, playing, all the things they once enjoyed, and their eating and sleeping habits often change.

Once a vet has ruled out a medical cause, the best treatment is to increase exercise, play, social interaction and companionship and after a few weeks or months, most dogs make a full recovery from this stressful period in their lives. It is important to address the problem early, otherwise it can become entrenched and require medication on top of the social interventions. John Ciribassi, past president of the American Veterinary Society of Animal Behaviour advises: 'Keep them engaged, do more of the things they like to do, get them a little more exercise, and they should be fine'.

SIGNS YOUR DOG IS

Unwell

Dogs can't use words to tell us that they are sick, so they can only let us know through physical symptoms and changes in behaviour. You know your dog better than anyone else, so if you have any suspicions about their health, however seemingly trivial, trust your instincts and speak to your vet.

First, it's worth noting that your dog may be living with pain without your knowledge. Although they have low sensitivity to pain, most dogs will soldier on because in the wild, showing weakness makes an animal vulnerable to attack. 'Canines have inherited an instinct to hide any pain that is caused by injury or infirmity,' says Stanley Coren in *Do Dogs Dream?* 'They hide their pain … but unfortunately this instinctive behaviour makes it difficult for we humans to recognise when our dogs are hurting'.

Generally, dogs in acute pain are more subdued than normal and may hide away and have stiff body movements or be unwilling to move. If you accidentally step on a dog's tail, he will yelp – that's the customary response to a sudden pain, but with prolonged acute pain, a dog will lie down, remain still and may whine quietly. Excessive licking, panting and drooling are signs of fear and stress, but also of pain. Dogs feeling milder pain or discomfort are more likely to pace around rather than stay still.

The top 16 signs that your dog may be ill

1. Bad breath, panting or drooling

2. Excessive drinking or urination

3. Appetite change – unexplained weight loss or gain

4. General lethargy, reduction in energy/activity level, lack of interest

5. Sleeping more than usual

6. Lameness or stiffness

7. Coughing, sneezing, laboured breathing

8. Skin complaints, hair loss, sores, lumps

9. Frequent vomiting or change in bowel movements

10. Dry, red, or cloudy eyes

11. Runny eyes or nose

12. Black stool, contains blood or mucus

13. Difficulty urinating or defecating

14. Shaking of the head

15. Excessive licking

16. Red or swollen gums

The above symptoms are all signs of underlying illness, but you should also be alert to other injuries that require emergency treatment, such as snake bites, poisoning, etc.

Bee or wasp sting: A bee stings only once but its barbed sting lodges in the skin and must be removed to prevent infection. Wasps can sting multiple times, making them potentially more dangerous. Stings generally cause localised irritation and swelling, which is usually mild and lasts a few hours, but call a vet immediately if you observe any of these signs of allergy: swelling around the mouth, throat, neck or head, difficulty breathing, weakness, or collapse.

Snake bite: Unless your dog yelps, the first signs of a snake bite usually include restlessness and excessive panting and drooling, although you might be able to locate the bite through redness, bleeding or swelling. If you do happen to see the snake, have a good look or take a photograph if you can do so safely (so the vet knows which anti-venom to administer), then get your dog to the emergency vet immediately. If the snake is poisonous, your dog may experience vomiting, diarrhoea, shock, collapse, seizures and sometimes paralysis while you are rushing him for treatment.

Poisoning: Dozens of house and garden plants are poisonous to dogs, as well as other common hazards around the home such as chocolate, grapes, raisins, onions, garlic, chives, alcohol, coffee beans, blue cheese, macadamia nuts, walnuts, pistachios, pecans, Niger bird seeds, slug pellets, Vitamin D tablets and human drugs (and anything mouldy so keep your dog away from your food waste bin). Some of those hazards may surprise you but this list is by no means exhaustive, so spend half an hour now on the internet to brush up your knowledge. It could save your dog's life.

Symptoms of poisoning vary depending on the type and quantity of the poison that has been ingested, but they include: agitation, drooling, panting, nausea, oral irritation, vomiting, diarrhoea, pale gums, heart issues, excessive bruising or bleeding, unsteadiness on feet, drowsiness, breathing problems, tremors, or convulsions. Needless to say, speedy treatment is paramount.

Some of those hazards may surprise you but this list is by no means exhaustive

ELDERLY DOGS

It used to be easy to work out a dog's age compared to humans. You simply multiplied their biological age by seven. However, with recent studies involving changes in DNA over time, the seven-year rule has now been widely discredited as a misconception.

Scientists now use epigenetics – the study of changes in organisms caused by modification of gene expression – to gain a more accurate picture of how dogs age in comparison to humans. It appears that dogs age very rapidly in the first two years, and slow down as they get older.

In a recent study, published in the journal *Cell Systems*, researchers found the first eight weeks of a dog's life are comparable to the first nine months of human infancy, but the ratio changes over time. Researchers at the University of California have even made the claim that puppies are middle-aged by the time they are two, are roughly equivalent to a 50-year-old human by the age of three, and then they age more slowly in later life. This analysis was based on measuring changes in DNA in 104 Labradors aged between four weeks and 16 years old.

According to *The Independent* newspaper, the research showed: 'By the age of two, the Labrador DNA was equivalent to a human in their early forties, rather than a 14-year-old human, which the traditional formula would suggest. However, ageing slows in dogs over time, meaning that by the age of 10, a Labrador is similar to a person aged 68.'

The ageing process depends on a variety of factors including breed, genetics and health issues. It's worth noting that the study doesn't take into account that smaller breeds tend to live longer than larger breeds. Here is a graph based on the results:

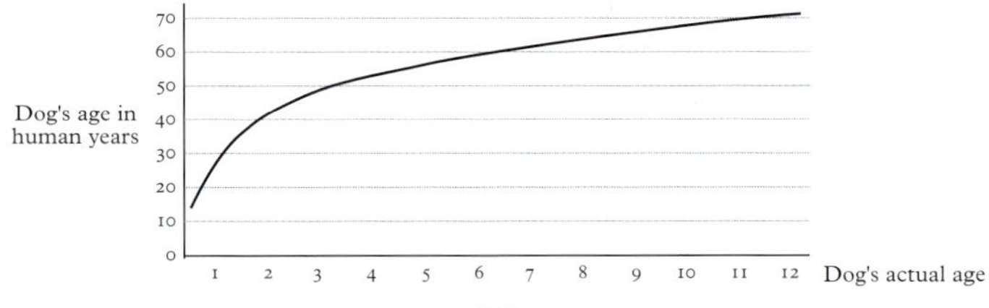

Despite all the scientific wrangling over human-equivalency, generally, dogs over seven should be considered seniors and their needs usually change from this age. Here are some important tips to keep your senior dog happy and healthy:

Diet: Good nutrition from birth is important for a long and healthy life, but it becomes especially important in the senior years. Typically, senior dog food will have more fibre content and less fat, plus some added ingredients to help the joints. Some senior diets have less protein, less phosphorus and a lower calorie content, but talk to your vet about your own dog's specific requirements and whether you should switch to a senior food.

Dental health: Look after their teeth and gums. Tartar build up in canines can have a lot of negative results.

Exercise: Just because your dog is old, it doesn't mean she shouldn't have regular exercise, even if it means shorter, slower walks rather than the epic hikes you might have enjoyed together in the past. Let your dog dictate the pace.

Obesity: Ageing is typically associated with lower energy expenditure and the tendency to gain fat and lose muscle, but it is important to maintain your dog at a healthy weight. Obesity puts more stress on the joints and it's associated with a range of health problems, just as with humans.

Temperature control: Older dogs are typically more sensitive to extreme temperature changes because of changes in their metabolism. They are less able to thermoregulate, just like older humans.

For more information about caring for a senior dog, see *Good Old Dog: Expert Advice for Keeping Your Aging Dog Healthy, Happy and Comfortable* edited by Nicholas Dodman.

WHAT CAN WE LEARN FROM DOGS?

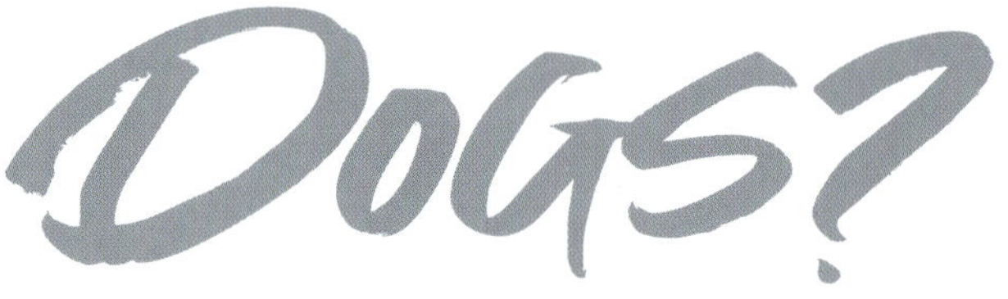

We have already discussed on page 16 that mutual domestication creates the possibility that both dogs and humans have evolved into less aggressive and more tolerant species as a result of our unique relationship. But our dogs can also teach us daily lessons about how to live our lives.

Be loyal: From Odysseus' faithful dog, Argos, and Fido the Italian street dog to Greyfriars Bobby and Hachikō the Japanese Akita, numerous heart-warming tales and true stories of loyal dogs from around the world are testament to their most abiding quality. The devotion and fidelity of our precious canine pets is deeply humbling and teaches us the true meaning of friendship.

Play: No matter how old they are, all dogs love to play and to invite others to join in the fun. We all know how important it is for our pet dogs to have regular exercise and lots of play, while we neglect ourselves and prioritise everything else. Dogs know that play is good for mind, body and soul and they don't let us forget it.

Keep it real: Dogs don't try to be something that they aren't and they don't care what other people think of them. No one looks at a dog and thinks, 'Mmm, but I wonder what he's really like, when he drops his guard, stops the showboating and allows you to really get to know him'. Dogs gain our trust and affection by always being themselves.

Live in the moment: Dogs literally follow their noses and they don't worry about today or tomorrow, they just make the most of every moment. They never waste their time wishing they were somewhere else doing something better and they never suffer from FOMO – Fear Of Missing Out – because there is always plenty of fun to be had right where they are!

Forgive: Your dog sits wide eyed, patiently waiting for you to give him a corner of your toast but this time he doesn't get any. Does he slink off to a corner to plot his revenge? Of course not. He trots blithely away and soon stumbles upon another opportunity to find happiness.

Show compassion: When you are feeling sad, your dog is the first to notice. He'll either come to you and spend some quiet time sharing your sadness, or else he'll try to lift you out of your deep blue funk with an invitation to play. Either way, he understands that you are hurting, so he clears his schedule because he wants to help.

Greet friends and family with enthusiasm: When was the last time you came home and your dog didn't even bother to drag himself over to say hello? When he was ill, that's when. At all other times he rushes to greet you with a helicopter tail and an infectious excitement that makes you smile and leaves you in no doubt that he really cares about you.

Love unconditionally: It doesn't matter how you look, how much you earn, how smart or interesting you are, what car you drive or clothes you wear, whether you've got killer abs or a muffin top, or if you feel totally unlovable, your dog will love you just the same.

Pay attention: You might learn something. Dogs have evolved to have unique social attentiveness towards humans, which is how they are able to learn and gain our trust. Humans can learn so much from each other so long as we are receptive and give people with whom we interact our undivided attention.

Accept yourself: Just as your dog loves you unconditionally, despite all your imperfections, he also doesn't waste his time longing to be taller, thinner or better looking. Does a Yorkshire Terrier mooch around wishing he was an Alaskan Malamute?

If you're happy and you know it, show it: When a dog is happy, he tells the whole world about it. When was the last time you actually jumped for joy? If your dog could speak, he would probably answer, 'about ten minutes ago'.